MAC 2000

Cartoons from the *Daily Mail*

Stan McMurtry **mac**

Edited by Mark Bryant

EQUINOX PUBLISHING LIMITED

To Nick and Katie

First published by Equinox Publishing Ltd 2000

Equinox Publishing Ltd
Edgware House,
389 Burnt Oak Broadway,
Edgware, Middlesex HA8 5TX
E-mail: Volliver@hotmail.com

Selection and text © Mark Bryant 2000

© Stan McMurtry

ISBN 1 903644 01 0

Typeset by Palimpsest Book Production Limited, Polmont, Stirlingshire

Printed and bound by Guernsey Press Limited

A test-case ruling by the European Court of Justice held that it was unlawful to discriminate against transsexuals in the armed forces. Meanwhile, an official report revealed that British surgeons worked more hours than safety guidelines allowed.

'If you worked the hours that I do, you'd make the occasional mistake too. Now, what is it? Stitches too tight?'

3 August 1999

The European Commission finally lifted its ban on British beef imposed in 1996 because of the BSE crisis. When Germany and France refused to accept the judgement, farmers' leaders called for Government action.

mac

'Damn! Searchlights and ack-ack guns. Jerry must be expecting us.'

5 August

After experts declared that Cornwall would be the best part of the country to witness the first total eclipse of the sun visible in Britain for 72 years, thousands headed south. In the event poor visibility marred the short-lived phenomenon for many.

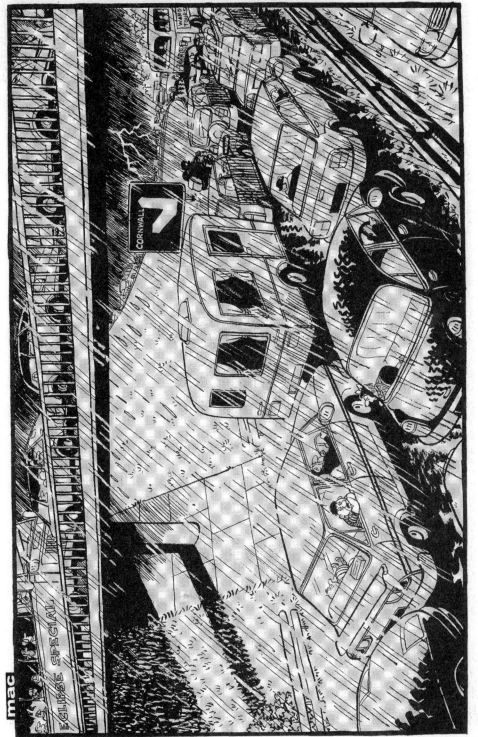

'Isn't it exciting? We're all rushing down there hoping that the sun will come out so we can watch it disappear again for two minutes on Wednesday.' *9 August*

A supermarket price-war began when American giant Wal-Mart took over Asda and immediately slashed prices in many top brand-name products. The British counter-offensive was spearheaded by market-leaders Tesco.

'Right, darling. Cornflakes, eggs, butter, custard powder and a cucumber. I'll call in at Asda on the way home.'

10 August

Farmers criticized the Government for naming sites of four new trials of genetically modified crops in Britain after fields had been destroyed by protesters angered at the growing of what they saw as potentially dangerous 'Frankenstein Food'.

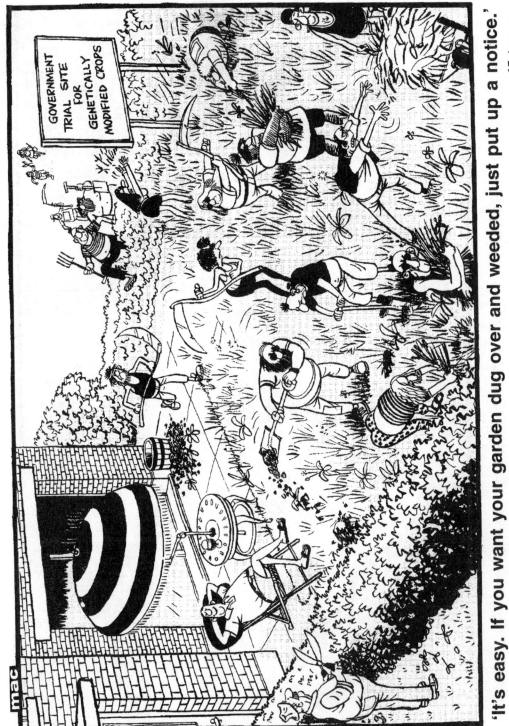

'It's easy. If you want your garden dug over and weeded, just put up a notice.'

17 August

A court in Middlesex heard how two Malaysians working for a Far Eastern betting syndicate sabotaged pitch floodlighting to halt play at advantageous points in two British Premiership football matches.

mac

'Ooh look, everybody. A big bunny rabbit.'

19 August

Newly appointed rail regulator Tom Winsor threatened Railtrack with fines of up to £40 million when a report revealed a 22% increase in late-running trains over the last 12 months with nearly one in ten trains in Britain failing to arrive on time.

'Right, Cyril. Commence new boarding procedure . . . reduce speed to 60mph . . . passenger pick-up net out . . . stand by . . .'

20 August

In a television interview, Shadow Home Secretary Ann Widdecombe claimed that the Prime Minister was using his position to get free holidays, after it was reported that the Blair family had moved from a luxury villa in Italy to a French château.

'It was a nice thought and I know you meant well, but tell those friends you met in Italy we don't want Ann Widdecombe in our swimming-pool.'

23 August

There was panic in Cornwall when anglers spotted a 16-foot great white shark off Padstow Bay. This was the first reported sighting in British coastal waters of the man-eating fish which had terrorized bathers in the Hollywood blockbuster *Jaws*.

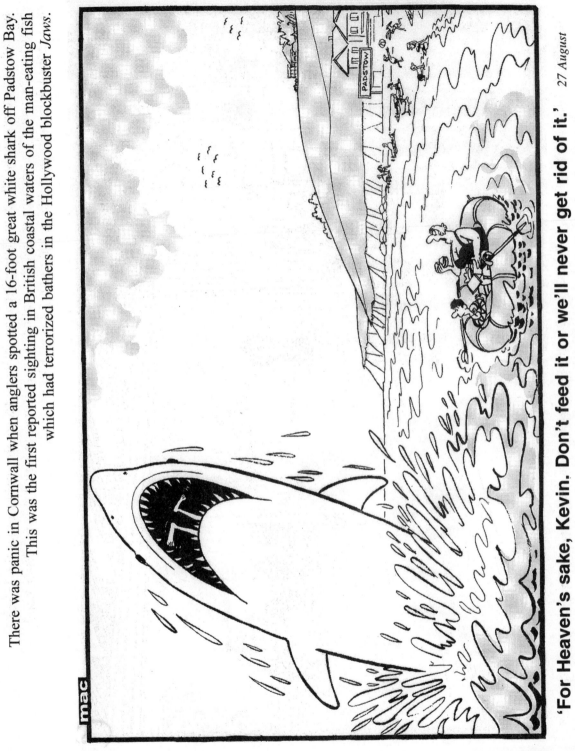

'For Heaven's sake, Kevin. Don't feed it or we'll never get rid of it.' *27 August*

Foreign Secretary Robin Cook was widely criticized when he invited Indonesian officials to visit the UK's largest arms fair after the regime had used British Hawk fighters to attack East Timor in the run-up to the area's independence referendum.

mac

'It's all right. The Indonesians have promised me on their honour they just want them to keep down the pigeon population in Jakarta.' 2 September

The Prime Minister accused Tory leader William Hague of undermining the peace process in Northern Ireland when he called on Ulster Secretary Mo Mowlam to halt prisoner releases until Sinn Fein and the IRA stopped 'flouting their obligations'.

mac

'It's for you, Mr Blair. Probably William Hague trying to undermine the peace process again.'

3 September

In the wake of news that two 12-year-old girls in South Yorkshire had become mothers, Tony Blair called on parents to join the Government in a moral crusade to stamp out teenage pregnancies.

mac

'Tony Blair says us parents should teach a sense of morality to our children – so you be a good girl, d'you hear?'

A storm of controversy broke when a leaked document revealed that a number of wealthy businessmen who had recently been ennobled, or received other honours from the Government, had also donated funds to the Labour Party.

'. . . So I says to my mate, Shamus back at the mission, what am I goin' to do with me lottery win? Why not make a donation to the Labour Party he says . . .'

7 September

After the death of Alan Clark, the maverick Tory ex-minister and MP for Kensington and Chelsea, there was much speculation that former Defence Secretary Michael Portillo, seen by many as a potential Tory Party leader, would stand for his seat.

'He's absolutely inconsolable, doctor. I had no idea William was so fond of Alan Clark.'

In announcing that he would stand for re-election Michael Portillo also admitted that he had had homosexual experiences as a student. This followed recent revelations about the sexuality of Labour politicians Chris Smith, Peter Mandelson and others.

'Look, darling. Isn't it exciting? – I think our Kevin's going into politics.'

10 September

The *Times* serialized a new book by KGB defector Vasili Mitrokhin in which it was revealed that Melita Norwood, an 87-year-old suburban great-grandmother, had been a Russian spy for four decades.

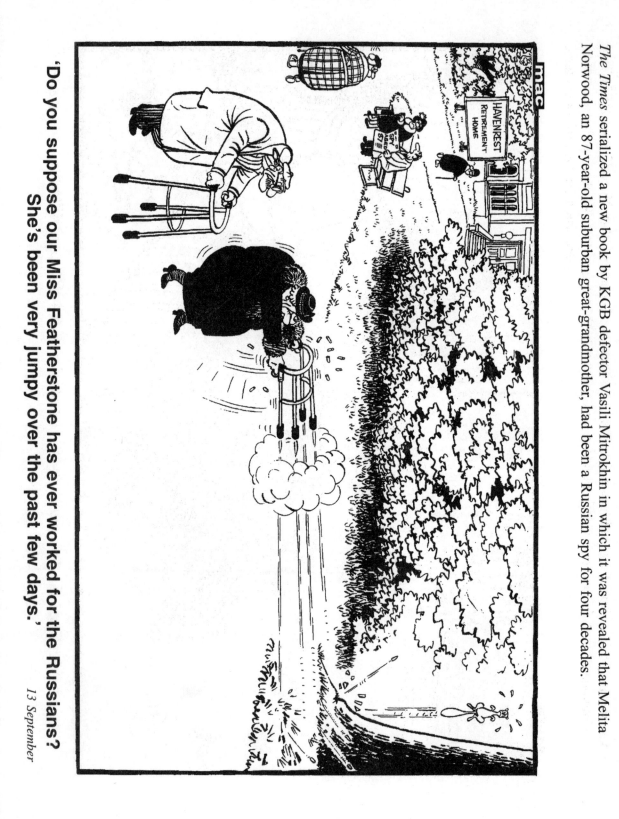

'Do you suppose our Miss Featherstone has ever worked for the Russians? She's been very jumpy over the past few days.'

13 September

A report in the *New York Post* said that during her bid to become Senator of New York 50-year-old Hillary Clinton, wife of the adulterous US president, had spent $3000 on a visit to a Manhattan plastic surgeon renowned for face-lift operations.

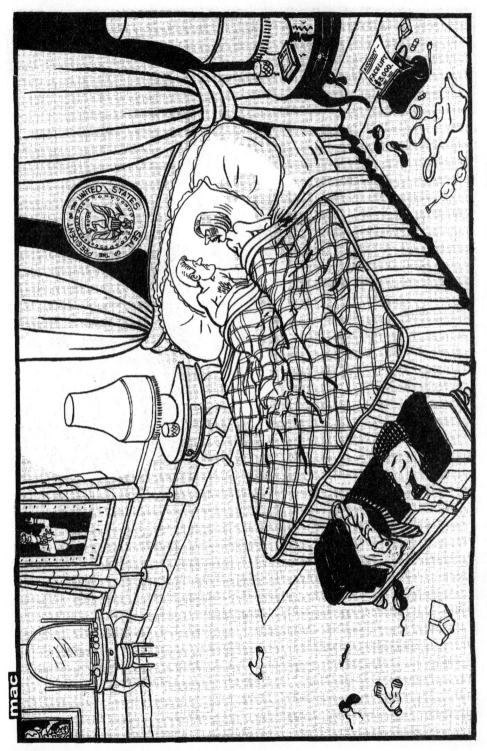

'What d'you mean, not a word to Hillary? I am Hillary!'

14 September

Speaking to the British Association's conference in Sheffield, a UFO expert from the Royal Astronomical Society announced that most sightings of so-called 'flying saucers' were actually of lenticular clouds, weather balloons etc.

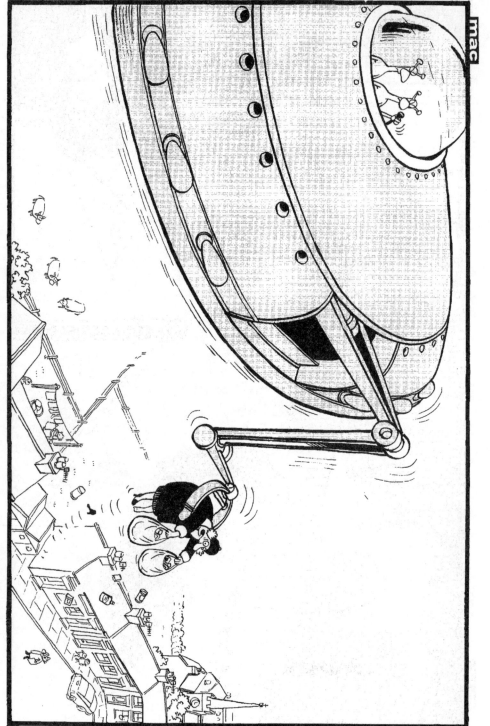

mac

'Don't panic, Doris. UFO scientists say it's just something called a lenticular cloud.'

The last volume in Colin Dexter's popular 'Inspector Morse' series of crime thrillers was published. In it the irascible, heavy-drinking Oxford detective – portrayed in the highly successful tie-in TV series by John Thaw – dies of kidney and heart failure.

'**Dammit, Mavis, you haven't gone and buried the telly?**'

17 September

Soon after the discovery of the Soviet great-grandmother spy, newly available files revealed that agents for East Germany's Stasi secret police had also been recruited in Britain.

'When you phoned you said your Gran was suspiciously swallowing her letters after reading them. Now you think it might've been toast?'

20 September

Despite strong opposition from countryside groups, Prime Minister Tony Blair pressed ahead with plans for a vote in the House of Commons on a bill to ban hunting with hounds but stressed that he had no intention of outlawing shooting or fishing.

'Get ready, Rodney. As soon as he's on the hook, shoot the little perisher!'

21 September

In an attempt to reduce car crime in Britain by 30% over the next five years, Home Secretary Jack Straw introduced a new scheme which would make it illegal for cars to be driven without an alarm or immobilizer being fitted.

mac

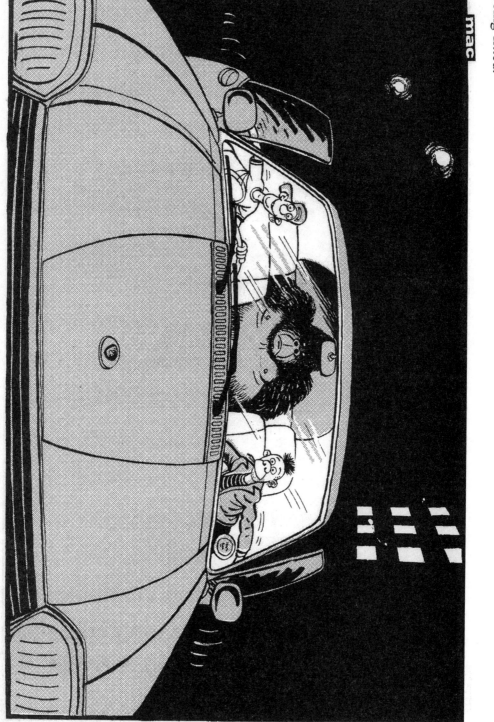

'Some people deserve to have their cars nicked.
Look at this, Wayne – no immobilizer!'

After a test case involving four sacked gay British service personnel, the European Court of Human Rights in Strasbourg ruled that homosexuals should be allowed to serve in Britain's armed forces.

'Oh, cooee! You with the big brown eyes and curly hair. Move away from your friends, sweetie. I'm going to throw a hand-grenade.'

28 September

At the Labour Party Conference in Bournemouth Education Secretary David Blunkett announced a crackdown on truancy, with parents facing fines of up to £2500 each or prison sentences for failing to keep their children at school.

mac

'Aw, bless 'im. His first day at school.'

30 September

Newly appointed Ulster Secretary Peter Mandelson – who had resigned from the Cabinet after admitting he had bought a house with a £373,000 loan from then Paymaster-General Geoffrey Robinson – moved into his official residence, Hillsborough Castle.

'Oh please, Geoffrey. Just a small loan. I've found this darling little place just a few miles from the office . . .'

12 October

When France continued to ignore the EU directive on British beef – declaring that because of the five-year incubation period of BSE it was unsafe until 2001 – the major UK supermarket chains began a boycott of French apples and other goods.

'Me too. It goes against all my principles, but right now I can't think of a British alternative.'

14 October

The 443-foot-high British Airways London Eye, the biggest revolving wheel in the world and the fourth tallest structure in the capital, was finally lifted into its upright position on the south bank of the Thames nearly opposite the Houses of Parliament.

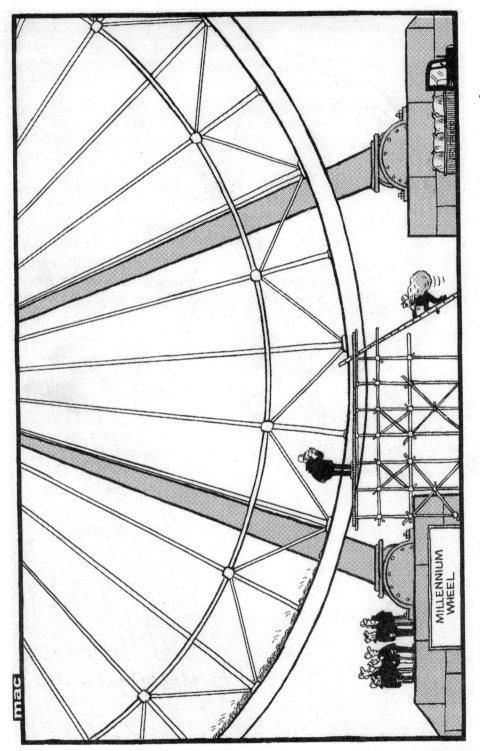

'Damn! It's still not moving – Cyril, six more sacks of hamsters.'   *18 October*

Shadow Home Secretary Ann Widdecombe attacked Jack Straw's pledge to recruit 5000 new police officers as 'smoke and mirrors dealing' when a leaked Treasury document revealed that more personnel were leaving the force than joining it.

'Don't cause any trouble, sunshine. There are two of us – gottle o' geer, gottle o' geer . . .'

Chinese President Jiang Zemin attended a banquet hosted by the Queen during his controversial state visit to Britain. Meanwhile, Prince Edward launched his new book, *Crown and Country*, which was tied in to a TV series of the same name.

'... and this room is where my son Edward will be happy to sign 30 million copies of his book for your people back home. Velly cheap.'

21 October

This year's shortlist for the annual £20,000 Turner Prize for modern art included *My Bed*, featuring 36-year-old artist Tracey Emin's own bed, complete with soiled sheets and underwear, cigarette-ends, empty vodka bottles and old newspapers.

mac

'Wake up, Norman. You've been nominated for the Turner Prize.' *22 October*

As the beef row continued to make headlines it emerged that 80% of industrially reared French livestock were routinely fed drugs, hormones, growth-activators and antibiotics banned by the EU.

'Zut alors! Look what you 'ave done. Now zey are stealing to feed their habit!'

25 October

The Department of Health announced that it had given the go-ahead for the world's first ever clinically proven anti-baldness pill, Propecia, which could be available on prescription in Britain before Christmas.

'Darling, there's been a bit of a mix-up. Those aren't your new baldness pills, they're Lucinda's Smarties.'

26 October

Anger over the ban on British beef was inflamed still further when it was revealed that 'fillers' derived from human excrement and sewage from septic tanks had been discovered in French cattle feed.

'*Mon Dieu*, Yvette. Caviare, pheasant, asparagus tips and delicious vegetables all washed down with a vintage Chablis – we spoil those cows.' *28 October*

25 years after the Rt Hon. Richard John Bingham, 7th Earl of Lucan, went missing following the brutal killing of his family's nanny and the attempted murder of his wife at their Belgravia home, the High Court officially declared him dead.

mac

'By Jove! We've got something to celebrate today, Lucan old chap. You've been declared officially dead.'

The Prime Minister, who had pledged to end hunting with hounds, had a personal meeting with the Prince of Wales at St James's Palace after Prince Charles took 17-year-old Prince William fox-hunting with the Beaufort Hunt in Gloucestershire.

'I promise you, Prime Minister. You won't know the thrill till you've experienced it. – All right, Withers. Release the cat.'

2 November

British surgeons at the North Hampshire Hospital in Basingstoke became the first in Europe to pioneer the use of voice-activated computers to perform hands-free operations.

'Hang on, Chief Surgeon. Go back to your golf.
The patient isn't on the operating table yet . . .'

4 November

In the Australian referendum on retaining the Queen as their head of state Her Majesty won by a narrow margin, with 45.3% voting in favour of a president appointed by politicians.

'It's all right. They've seen sense. You can release Rolf Harris.' *8 November*

Chancellor Gordon Brown's autumn Budget announced regular £100 winter heating allowances for OAPs and free TV licences for older pensioners.

'Better not touch it, Ethel. It's probably our winter heating.'

11 November

A newly appointed 32-year-old drama teacher at a Worcestershire boarding-school was acquitted of seducing a 15-year-old boy on a field trip to Wales but sacked for swimming naked in the sea in front of pupils while drunk.

'Cooee, boys. Biology homework – anyone for skinny-dipping?'

12 November

A 'postcode lottery' over Health Service funding of expensive drugs for killer diseases was discovered, with some patients having to buy their own medicines for cancer and other illnesses while neighbouring health authorities provided these on the NHS.

'That's the deal, Mr Hetherington. You operate on this and then we'll operate on you.'

As the Millennium loomed, novelist and former Tory Chairman Lord Archer was forced to abandon his bid to become Mayor of London and was expelled from the Conservative Party when a long-silent key witness in his 1987 libel battle spoke out.

'The Millennium? Oh, Jeffrey's thinking of going off somewhere quiet to write another book.'

29 November

In a new effort to help solve crime, the Prime Minister promised an extra £17 million a year to Britain's police forces to carry out DNA tests on those convicted of all but the most minor offences.

'See that little blue vein there, Hoskins? I think you have to aim at that.'

The Scout Association threatened legal action and demanded a public apology after 52-year-old Sir Elton John performed with a troupe of male strippers dressed as Cub Scouts at a musical benefit for gay rights group Stonewall at the Royal Albert Hall.

'And now, Mr Featherstone our Scoutmaster will sing "Oh, I'm Happy Being Hetero" whilst the Cubs dance around a campfire made of old Elton John wigs . . .'

2 December

After widespread criticism, Deputy Prime Minister John Prescott handed over control of transport policy to his deputy, Lord Macdonald, but declared that he would still remain in overall charge of the department.

'Yes, yes, Mr Prescott's still in overall charge . . . hang on a minute . . . thanks, just put it down there will you?'

14 December

The European Court of Human Rights ruled that former Home Secretary Michael Michael Howard had had no authority to increase the prison sentences of the two 10-year-old killers of toddler James Bulger in 1993 and that their human rights had been violated.

17 December

Human Rights Violated, 1993

Hard on the heels of the Jeffrey Archer affair and the fiasco of whether or not to allow Steven Norris to run for London Mayor, the defection of Shaun Woodward to the Labour Party cast fresh doubts on William Hague's qualities as Tory leader.

'Aw, c'mon. Things could be worse. You could be William Hague.' *21 December*

Former Tory minister Neil Hamilton faced financial ruin after losing his libel battle against Mohamed Al Fayed over the cash-for-questions scandal and claims that he and his wife had enjoyed luxurious hospitality and food at Harrods and the Paris Ritz.

'Everything gone? I told you not to let the Hamiltons in first.' *23 December*

Prompted by his wife Cherie, the Prime Minister had his eyes tested and began to appear in public wearing trendy oval-shaped Calvin Klein designer spectacles.

'Tony, dear. If you're going to switch the tree lights on, wear your new specs. We don't want to spoil Russia's Christmas, do we?'

24 December

After the extended Christmas and Millennium break it was back to work. The much-hyped four-mile-long, 'River of Fire' London fireworks feature travelled from Tower Bridge to Vauxhall Bridge so quickly that few of those lining the route saw it.

'Here it comes – the river of fire.'

4 January 2000

A virulent flu epidemic left hospitals crowded, with only 11 NHS intensive-care beds available in the whole of England. Such was the chaos that doctors at a hospital in Harrow had to examine patients in a St John's Ambulance Brigade bus in the carpark.

mac

'How are you, mother? Hospital still as crowded as ever?'

7 January

Britain finally adopted the EU ruling on gays serving in the armed forces. Meanwhile, the Home Secretary made a controversial decision not to allow the ageing Chilean dictator, General Augusto Pinochet, to be extradited from the UK on health grounds.

'All these months I've been longing to tell you, Augusto. Inside this policeman's uniform there's a military man like you, longing to come out . . .'   *13 January*

The science journal *Nature* published the results of a study by a professor of evolutionary psychology at the University of Liverpool which seemed to indicate that taller men are more attractive to women.

'Oh, Norman. You shouldn't have!'

Dr Mo Mowlam, Cabinet Office Minister and head of the Government's anti-drugs campaign, admitted on Sky TV that she had smoked cannabis while on a postgraduate course in Iowa, USA, in the 1970s.

'I must say meeting you is quite a surprise, Dr Mowlam.
You're much taller than I was expecting.'

18 January

Supermarket chain Tesco announced that it would triple the number of its stores offering Internet access following the huge increase in demand since it launched its on-line shopping service, Tesco Direct, a year ago.

mac

'Talk me through it, Eileen. Which keys did you press today?'

21 January

Defence Secretary Geoff Hoon faced intense questioning in the House of Commons when leaked reports revealed that cash-strapped navy chiefs had been ordering large numbers of warships to stay in port to cut down on fuel bills.

'Don't get angry, old chap. We just need enough to get back to port.' *24 January*

A nationwide survey by the *Daily Mail* discovered that thousands of NHS patients still shared mixed wards despite a Government election promise in 1997 that 70% of health authorities would have been made to abandon the practice within two years.

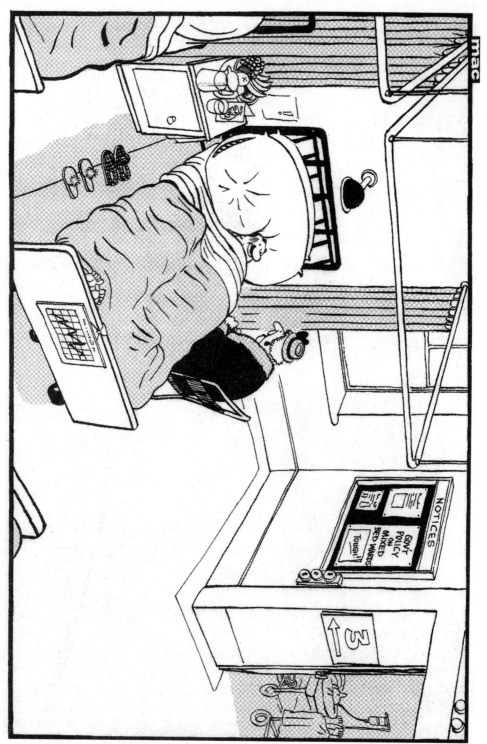

'Well, I must say you're looking much better. Your cheeks are all aglow.'

After a legal challenge from a female cancer victim, the Government's Human Fertility & Embryology Authority lifted its ban on the 'freeze-thaw' technique for the preservation of human eggs, opening the door for career women to have children later in life.

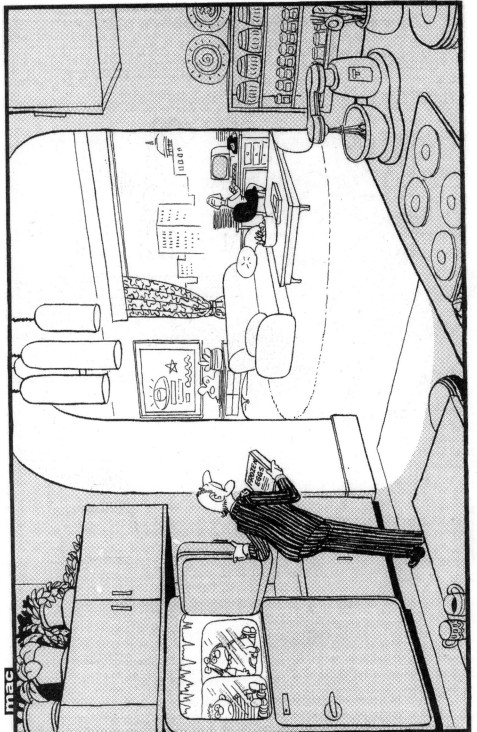

'I know you're frantically busy again Fiona, darling. But it distinctly says on the packet, "Do not re-freeze after thawing out"'.

27 January

In one of the most controversial episodes in the 49-year history of BBC Radio 4's farming soap, *The Archers*, single mother Jolene and married man Sid Perks — landlord of the Bull pub in Ambridge — appeared in a steamy naked shower scene.

'Well, showering together sounded dead sexy on *The Archers*. Maybe the bloke took his hat off and put his fag out.'

28 January

The Ulster peace process hung in the balance again when the Canadian General John de Chastelain, chairman of the independent panel examining arms decommissioning, reported that the IRA had done nothing to advance the hand-in of their weapons.

'They're still turning somersaults, lads. All our boys are out of prison, they've changed the RUC – sit tight and they might agree to world cruises and villas in Bermuda.'

1 February

The Countess of Wessex upset the Royal Family and anti-fur campaigners alike when she accepted lavish hospitality during a business weekend in St Moritz, Switzerland, and was photographed wearing a red fox-fur hat.

'Do you hear me, Sophie? Get back from St Moritz immediately and bring those furs with you.'

Pierre-Yves Gerbeau, a former vice-president of Disneyland Paris, was hired to replace the sacked chief executive of the ailing Millennium Dome. Though he announced a major shake-up he promised to leave the Dome's 14 zones untouched.

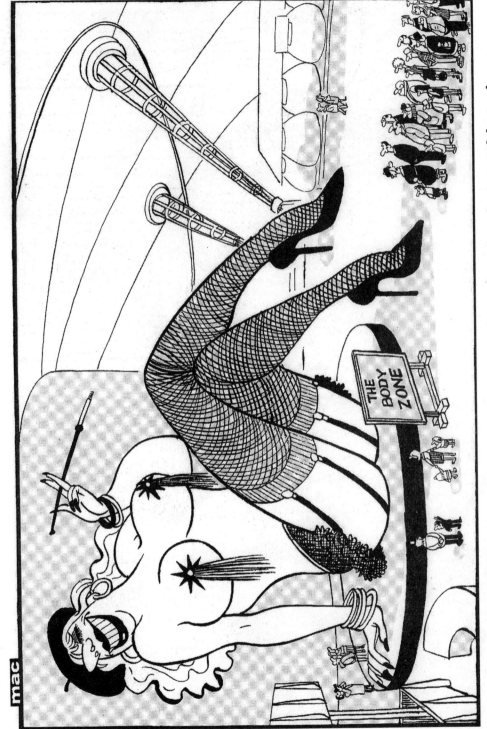

mac

THE BODY ZONE

'I thought that Frenchman said he wasn't going to change things.' *8 February*

Three hostages released from an Afghan plane which had been hijacked on a 40-minute internal flight from Kabul and forced to land at Stansted Airport, Essex, asked for political asylum in Britain.

mac

'Take us to Stansted!'

10 February

A 13-year-old girl who was repeatedly bullied at a 750-pupil comprehensive school in Bilborough, Nottinghamshire, was given a female teacher as a bodyguard when the school refused to expel her tormentors.

'Think carefully, Rachel. After your bodyguards put Samantha's feet into the bucket of concrete, then what did they do with her?'

18 February

24-year-old Manchester United and England soccer star David Beckham was dropped from his team's side in a match against Leeds when he failed to attend a training session because his wife had insisted he stay at home with her to look after their sick son.

'If there is a David Beckham in the ground, will he please return home immediately? His wife wants to go shopping.'

A Land Registry survey in England and Wales revealed a nationwide boom in house prices not seen since the 1980s, with some properties in London and the South rocketing in value by up to a third on their former prices.

'Oh, didn't she tell you? Your wife sold it to us this morning. She says she'll send you a card from Bermuda.'

25 February

A showbiz rally was held at the Old Vic Theatre, London, to celebrate the centenary of the founding of the Labour Party. Meanwhile, Ken Livingstone, defeated as the official Labour candidate for London Mayor, threatened to stand as an independent.

mac

LABOUR'S 100th BIRTHDAY

100 TODAY

'Are you sure you told him Ken Livingstone was going to burst out of the cake?'

As speculation grew over whether Prince Charles and Camilla Parker Bowles would get married, the Prince of Wales reached Jamaica on his official tour of the Caribbean.

'. . . and guess what, Camilla! They have the same customs as us – on February 29th in a leap year the women are allowed to propose.'

29 February

62-year-old Moors murderer, Ian Brady – who had been force-fed while on hunger strike at a high-security hospital – went to court to win the right to die. Meanwhile, the Prime Minister declared that press reports on the crisis in the NHS were alarmist.

'It must be a great consolation to know that the authorities are doing their utmost to keep Ian Brady alive.'

2 March

After a protracted court battle costing the British taxpayer £75 million – which included a 15-month stay at a luxury mansion on the exclusive Wentworth Estate in Virginia Water, Surrey – Chilean dictator General Pinochet finally flew home.

'Hello there. Remember me? Idi Amin. Ah understand there's a completely free holiday home just become vacant at Wentworth.'

3 March

Cherie Blair obtained a High Court injunction to prevent the *Mail on Sunday* publishing extracts from a book written by a former Downing Street nanny.

'Riveting. But will Blair allow it? – "I opened the door, he got in, I shut the door. Later, I opened the door, he got out, I shut the door. Next morning, I opened the door . . ."'

As Tony Blair declared that he wanted everyone in Britain to have easy access to the Internet within five years, a 'web war' broke out with many service-providers offering free subscriptions and other special deals.

'If anyone would like a cocoa before we go to bed, please contact:
wife.mother@kitchen.uk.'

9 March

Following the publication of a Government-sponsored report into the black economy by Lord Grabiner QC, Chancellor Gordon Brown announced a ruthless crackdown on tax and benefit cheats.

mac

'Oh gawd, Doreen. I've forgotten who I am next: Bert Simpson, unemployed plumber; Sharon Scaggs, single mother; or Sid Bainbridge with the bad back.'

10 March

Home Office Minister Paul Boateng revealed new measures to tackle East European gypsy street-beggars. Meanwhile, campaign managers desperately tried to improve the faltering image of the official Labour candidate for London Mayor, Frank Dobson.

'Trust me, Frank. It works in London. Just look sad, then in a pitiful whimper say, "Please spare a vote on May 4th".'

13 March

A 60-year-old Algerian asylum-seeker, together with his two wives and 15 children, received £32,000 in benefits, as well as free schooling and accommodation in two fully-furnished four-bedroomed houses with satellite TV, while their case was considered.

'What d'you mean, I'll want a house? I'll need a street, a primary school and somewhere comfy for the camels.'

14 March

Education Secretary David Blunkett announced plans to invite private companies to take over and run 75 ailing English inner-city secondary schools, which would thereafter be called 'academies'.

'Of all the private firms that could've taken over our ailing school, we had to get Dyno-Rod!'

16 March

After much discussion, Anglican and Catholic bishops agreed to the repeal of Clause 28 of the Local Government Act 1988, which banned the promotion of homosexuality in schools.

'How much longer are you going to spend praying for guidance on Clause 28, Godfrey? Get into bed, it's freezing!'

17 March

Manchester United and England soccer star David Beckham sported a 'number two' crew-cut for the first time at his club's match against Leicester City.

'Quick, Enid. I sold the lot. Where's the cat?'

20 March

In his Budget statement Chancellor Gordon Brown announced a dramatic increase in Health Service spending, with £19.4 billion a year promised to the NHS by 2003.

'That's right, Mrs Wetherby. We're going to spend, spend, spend, spend! So not only did we unblock your sinuses, we replaced your hips, removed your appendix and threw in a frontal lobotomy.'

23 March

A Downing Street spokesman confirmed that Cherie Blair, pregnant with her fourth child, had been encouraging the Prime Minister to take advantage of new EU rules granting fathers unpaid paternity leave when their baby was born.

24 March

'Funnily enough, Cherie and I were just discussing that — and yes, I think I will be taking paternity leave.'

The science journal *Nature* published the results of a survey by Dr Marc Breedlove of the University of California which suggested that if a man's index finger is shorter than his ring finger there is a greater chance of his being gay.

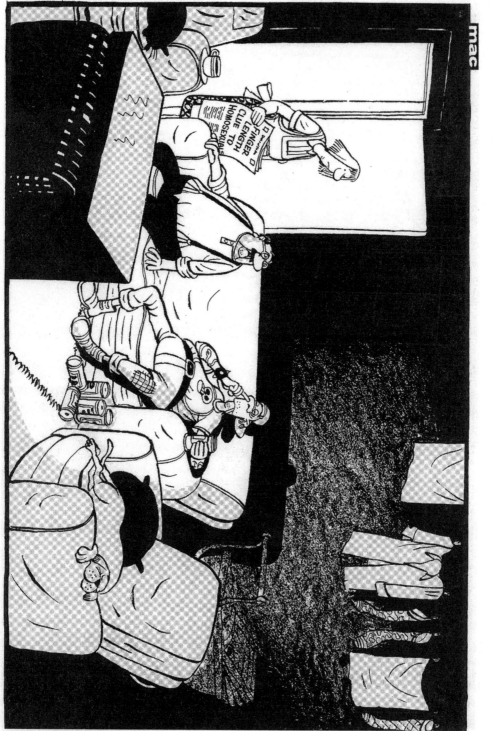

'Kevin, take your finger out a minute. Your mum wants to know your sexual orientation.'

The Queen and Prince Philip returned from their two-week tour of Australia the day after Mothering Sunday. Despite the recent close vote in the referendum on sovereignty they had received a warm welcome from monarchists and republicans alike.

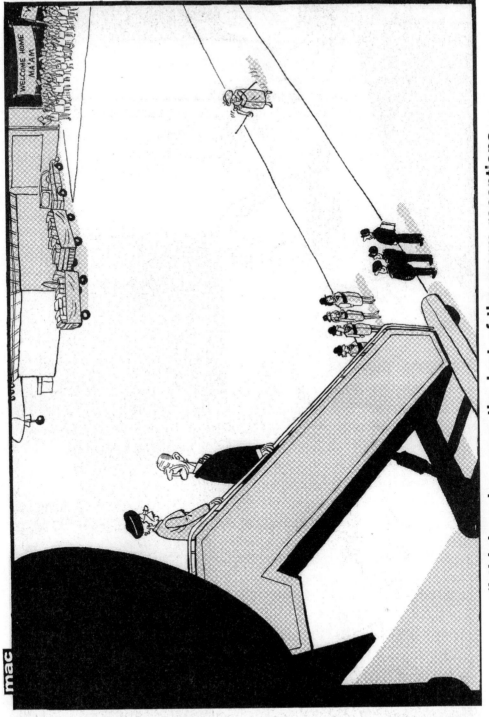

'I think we've seen the last of the warm receptions.
Did you forget to send a Mother's Day card?'

3 April

There was a public outcry when Barclays Bank sent 300,000 letters to customers – many of them living in isolated areas with no other banking facilities – announcing the closure of 172 of its branches, despite record profits of £1.89 billion last year.

'It's a train ticket to their nearest local branch in London.
Our account will be debited.'

4 April

Two high-earning British executives, both married and previously total strangers, were arrested and fined for having drunken sex during a film on a transatlantic flight from Dallas, Texas, to Manchester.

7 April

'Welcome home, darling. Good flight?'

After a frustrated British pensioner flew to India for a cataract operation, former Labour minister Frank Field suggested that NHS patients should be sent to Third World countries for surgery in an effort to cut hospital waiting-lists.

mac

'Before you start, are you absolutely sure you know where the appendix is?'

SURGERY

IN ASSOCIATION WITH THE FRANK FIELD OPERATIONS ABROAD NHS SCHEME.

Police officers in London's Royal Parks Constabulary were issued with roller-blade sports boots in an attempt to catch skating and cycling law-breakers in the capital.

'The roller-blades are for you, Hawkins. Not your horse!'

13 April

City traders braced themselves as London share prices plummeted after a huge fall on Wall Street. Meanwhile, the 20th London Marathon was won by Portugal's 34-year-old Antonio Pinto in a new European record time of 2 hours 6 minutes 36 seconds.

mac

'I'm sorry. Mr Simpkins is a very busy man. He's only just finished the London Marathon and now he's doing the high jump . . .'

17 April

The FTSE-100 index listing the value of the UK's top companies continued to fall as the investment bubble in on-line 'dotcom' enterprises burst. Meanwhile, Russian President Vladimir Putin visited Britain and had tea with the Queen at Windsor Castle.

'You're his interpreter. What on earth does "Damski blastski, footsy dot com updabluddyspout" mean?'

18 April

Britain's hard-hit farmers faced fines of up to £5000 for failure to comply with a new EU directive to identify all the UK's 44 million sheep by tattooing them on their heads with a code naming their farm of origin, in an effort to track the spread of diseases.

'So I said, "Hey man, don't mess about. If I'm going to have a tattoo I want the full works".'

20 April

On the eve of the vote for London's first elected mayor, peaceful anti-capitalism demonstrations turned into riots. The pollsters' favourite candidate, Ken Livingstone, who had previously supported 'direct action', denounced the violence.

"'Ear that, Wayne? Apparently all that was needed to make our mark for Ken was a little cross wiv a pencil.'"

4 May

A Yorkshire landlord who had barred a six-foot-tall transsexual from his village pub because she made the regulars feel uncomfortable had to pay £1000 in compensation in a court case over sex discrimination.

mac

"'Ello, handsome. I take it there are no objections to persons recently released from the torment of being trapped in men's bodies knocking back a few pints in your pub?'

5 May

There was a major breakthrough in the Ulster peace process when the IRA agreed to open up its weapons dumps to inspection by the former President of Finland, Martii Ahtisaari, and former African National Congress leader, Cyril Ramaphosa.

'Oh, stop fussing, woman! Nobody's going to notice you haven't dusted.' *8 May*

34-year-old Estée Lauder model Liz Hurley was photographed sucking a pink babies' dummy while on a Caribbean holiday. A spokesman later announced that she had bought it to help her give up smoking.

'These dummies are wonderful. I haven't heard a word from Enid since I told her she looks like Liz Hurley.'

9 May

The report of a Government inquiry into mobile phones was published and warned of the dangers of their use by children, who are more vulnerable to radiation emissions. Meanwhile, a survey stated that 430,000 cellphone users are aged between 7 and 16.

'Believe me. After a while the craving will stop. You'll feel healthier and able to talk without one . . .'

11 May

The Queen officially opened the Tate Modern gallery of modern art in the former Bankside power-station on the south bank of the Thames.

mac

'. . . and then I was shown a Damien Hirst animal sawn in half. Well, honestly. Even I could do that.'

12 May

Broadcasters hit the headlines when BBC chiefs refused to screen live coverage of the pageant to celebrate the 100th birthday of the Queen Mother because it clashed with *Neighbours*. Channel 5 was also criticized for showing too much soft porn.

'Wonderful news, everybody. I've just given exclusive rights to Channel 5 – But we've all got to take our clothes off.'

15 May

39-year-old TV presenter Carol Vorderman, who made her name as the maths wizard on the afternoon quiz show *Countdown*, attracted media attention at the BAFTA Awards ceremony in London when she arrived wearing a strapless mini-dress.

'The governors are confident that your mathematical teaching skills are every bit as good as Carol Vorderman's, Miss Winthrop – but there the resemblance must end.'

16 May

In the BBC's annual Reith Lecture on Radio 4, given this year by Prince Charles, the Prince argued in favour of organic farming, stressing the unknown dangers and 'potentially disastrous consequences' of growing genetically modified food.

'The shame of it, Camilla. Right in the middle of the Reith Lecture, my begonia confesses to me that she's been cross-pollinated by a genetically modified cucumber!'

18 May

45-year-old Cherie Blair gave birth to her fourth child, Leo, the first baby to be born to the wife of a serving Prime Minister for 150 years.

mac

'. . . so much for Labour's foreign policy, Leo. Now a word about what you've missed. Those years of Tory misrule over taxes, the Health Service and education. Furthermore . . . okay, Cherie, he's asleep now.'

22 May

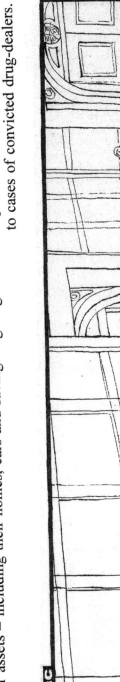

Cabinet Office Minister Mo Mowlam announced plans to allow judges to strip all convicted career criminals of their assets – including their homes, cars and savings – giving courts new powers formerly only applicable to cases of convicted drug-dealers.

'You heard me, sunshine. Hand over your wallet, your Rolex and your credit cards!'

23 May

The Millennium Commission agreed to give a further £29 million from Lottery funds to bail out the struggling Greenwich Dome on condition that its chairman, former British Airways chief executive Bob Ayling, was sacked.

'Better take the cart. The people at Greenwich say it's quite a big bit of scrap.'

25 May

In an equal opportunities drive, the Ministry of Defence announced that women in the armed forces would henceforward train for frontline fighting like men and that the possibility of lifting the ban on arming female personnel was also being considered.

'It must've been nice having your wife at home on leave for the Bank Holiday, George!'

30 May

Health Secretary Alan Milburn sent out 12 million leaflets to hospitals and supermarkets asking the public what improvements they would like to see in the National Health Service.

mac

'The Government have sent out millions of leaflets asking people how they would improve the NHS.'

1 June

The Queen finally gave official recognition to Camilla Parker Bowles as the consort of Prince Charles when she met and spoke to her at a party for ex-King Constantine of Greece which the Prince of Wales hosted at Highgrove House in Gloucestershire.

'It's Mrs Parker Bowles, Ma'am. Now that you've broken the ice, how do you fancy a girly night out down at her local?'

5 June

A flotilla of small boats accompanied war veterans to Dunkirk in France for a ceremony to mark the 60th anniversary of the evacuation of Allied troops. Meanwhile, there were fears of violence by English soccer fans in the run-up to Euro 2000.

'Fantastic! So you were losing this battle and they sent a flotilla of small boats – who were England playing, Grandad?'

In a surprise example of accidental cross-breeding, Molly, an 18-year-old goat, gave birth to a lamb at an animal sanctuary in the grounds of TV scriptwriter Carla Lane's Elizabethan manor house in West Sussex.

'Oh. Hi, girls!'

Despite attracting its biggest audience of the year, Channel 5 TV was heavily criticized when it screened *Naked Jungle*, a nude gameshow hosted by Keith Chegwin, as part of its season marking the 50th anniversary of naturism in Britain.

mac

'It must be another programme for Channel 5.'

9 June

Annual figures showed a dramatic fall in Labour's lead over the Tories and Tony Blair's personal image was badly dented after being heckled and slow-handclapped while addressing 10,000 members of the Women's Institute at Wembley Arena.

'Famous last words – "I've just thought how to become popular again, Cherie darling. How about another baby?"'

12 June

As the Euro 2000 football tournament began, Lord Burns' long-awaited Government report on hunting was published.

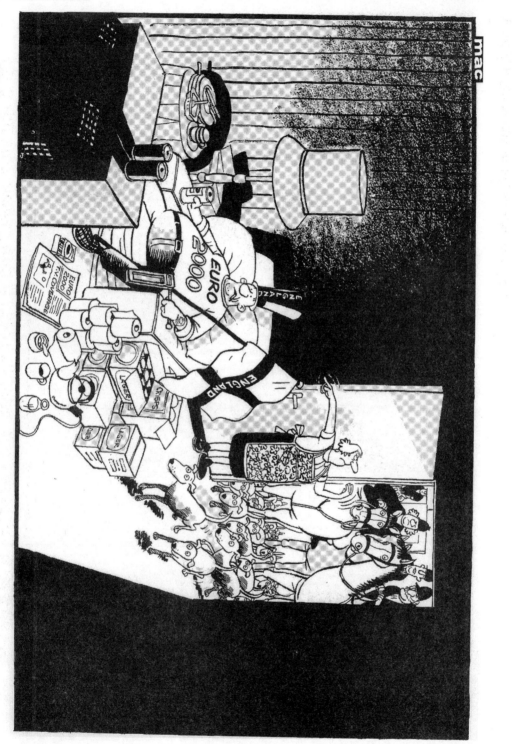

mac

'This fox-huntin' business, Marge. Can you imagine anyone wanting to watch one of God's creatures being ripped to pieces?'

13 June

England football fans were ecstatic when the national team beat arch-rivals Germany in a historic match during Euro 2000. However, the victory was marred by riots involving English supporters in Belgium, which led to 800 being deported.

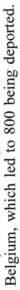

'Great match? Bleedin' 'ell, dad. I've had a busy week smashing up shops, fighting the police, gettin' deported. I 'aven't 'ad time to watch any football. – Who won?'

19 June

Only 24 hours after the bodies of 58 Chinese illegal immigrants were discovered in a lorry at Dover, nine Iranian stowaways caught travelling in a Belgian truck were detained by police. Meanwhile, the annual Royal Ascot horseracing event opened.

mac

'Now remember. If we get stopped when we enter Britain, just say: "What ho, old bean. We're just orf for a jolly old flutter on the gee-gees."'

22 June

Speaking at a Government-sponsored 'body-image summit', Women's Minister Tessa Jowell backed a plan to monitor the number of fat and thin women who appear on TV in an attempt to curb rising numbers of young women with eating disorders.

'. . . and now for the benefit of our young, impressionable female viewers, the next part of the news will be presented by a slightly plump and dumpy newsreader, followed shortly by an enormously fat one . . .' *23 June*

mac

28-year-old American Pete Sampras won Wimbledon for the seventh time and also entered the record books by winning his thirteenth Grand Slam title. Meanwhile, J.K. Rowling's fourth 'Harry Potter' children's book became an instant bestseller.

'Good news, Norman. You can be reunited with your wife and child – Wimbledon's over and your little girl's finished her Harry Potter book.'

10 July

Stung by claims that he was worn out by the combined pressures of office and his new baby, Tony Blair held a news conference in the state dining-room of Number 10 to trumpet the successes of New Labour since the General Election.

TRANSLATION: 'If you've woken me again to tell me the economy's booming, unemployment's down and how you're saving the country, I'll be sick all over your pyjamas!'

13 July

Buckingham Palace announced that Prince William and Prince Harry would not be attending the 100th birthday pageant for the Queen Mother in Horseguards Parade as they would be on holiday. One source speculated that they were going rock-climbing.

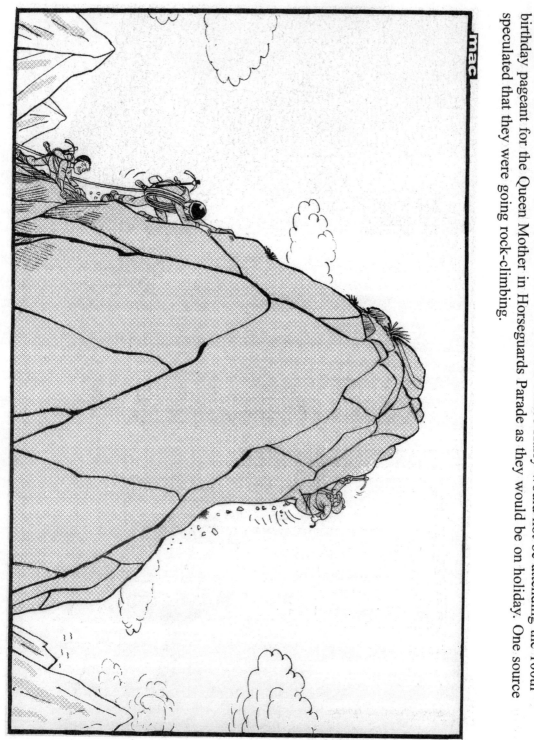

'I hope Great Great Gran wasn't too cross when she heard what we're doing instead of going to her pageant on Wednesday, Harry.'

There was an urgent investigation at Downing Street after the leak of a personal memorandum from Tony Blair to key aides admitting that the Government was out of touch with the public and requesting vote-pulling gimmicks to improve its image.

'Could you question the staff more quietly? Their screams keep waking Leo.'

18 July

Chancellor Gordon Brown launched the biggest public-sector spending spree since the war, with £43 billion promised over the next three years, including a £540 million cash boost to education, payable directly to headteachers and bypassing local councils.

mac

DUN TEACHIN

'I'd like to propose a toast, Headmaster – to Gordon Brown for sending the new school funding directly to you and for believing you'd spend it on books.'

20 July

Buoyed by a recent poll showing Labour in a commanding 19-point lead over the Conservatives, Tony Blair returned from the G8 economic summit in Okinawa, Japan, in an upbeat mood, despite the publication of more leaked Government documents.

'Believe me, Prime Minister, if anyone had tried to rifle through your wheelie-bin while you were in Japan, I would have noticed.'

24 July

Scientists at the Institute of Clinical Biochemistry discovered that a recently introduced police breath-test meter had consistently produced inaccurately high readings, leading to the possibility of thousands of convictions being quashed.

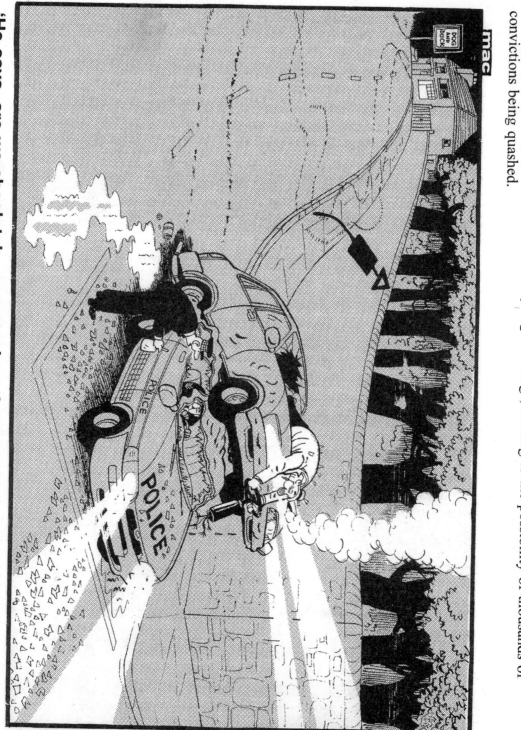

'He says, are we absolutely sure our breath-test equipment isn't faulty, Sarge?'

25 July

In a controversial Home Office shake-up of Britain's sex laws, gays were put on the same footing as heterosexuals, with 'cruising' for partners in public places and other practices no longer being deemed a criminal offence.

27 July

'I don't care what Jack Straw says – not here!'

The Government unveiled a ten-year strategy to bring the ailing NHS into the twenty-first century with the promise of 20,000 more nurses, 2000 more GPs, 7500 more consultants and 7000 more hospital beds by 2004.

'I knew there'd be a catch.'

Deputy Prime Minister John Prescott was at the centre of a new row when it was revealed that nearly £100,000 of taxpayers' money had been spent on refurbishing his official London residence, including £13,000 on a handwoven Wilton carpet.

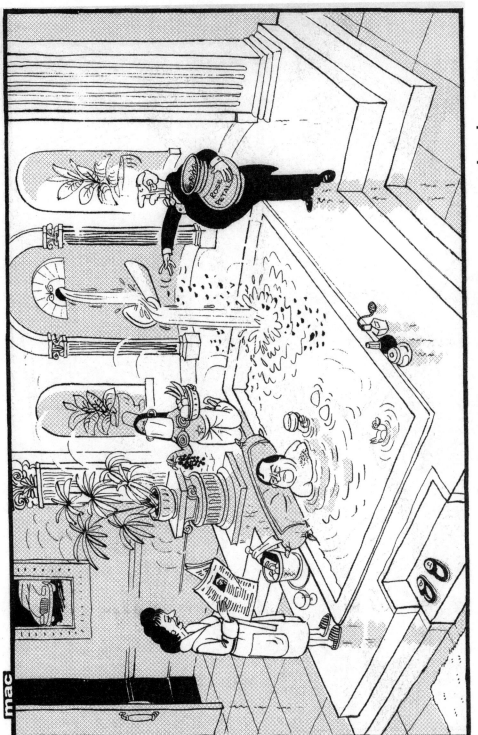

'Honestly, John. How petty-minded. The Tories are moaning because you've spent £13,000 on a new carpet.'

The first 'Dump the Pump' day was organized as a 24-hour nationwide boycott of petrol stations in a demonstration of public anger at the high price of fuel, 70% of which goes to the Chancellor of the Exchequer in duty.

mac

'You're fed up? Just think how fed up Gordon Brown is that we passed all those petrol stations back there.'

1 August

44-year-old Texan model and mother of four Jerry Hall took over the role of Mrs Robinson – which features a nude scene – in the stage version of *The Graduate* at the Gielgud Theatre in London's West End.

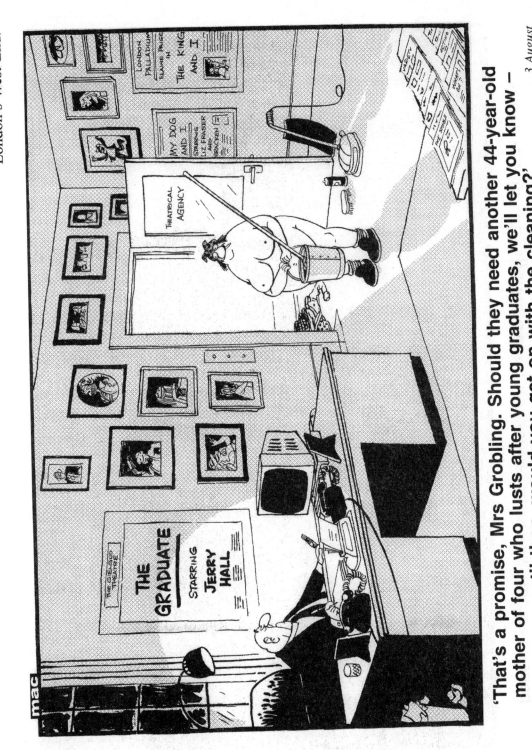

'That's a promise, Mrs Grobling. Should they need another 44-year-old mother of four who lusts after young graduates, we'll let you know – until then, would you get on with the cleaning?'

3 August

The Queen Mother celebrated her 100th birthday – the first member of the British Royal Family ever to do so – and, like all centenarians received a birthday message from the Queen.

'Your Majesty, the Queen Mother – this is your life!'

4 August

Angered by press photographers who took pictures at the christening of his son Leo, despite being asked not to do so, Tony Blair threatened to cancel a family photocall at his holiday villa in Tuscany, Italy. However, in the event he relented.

'Honestly, old chap. Cherie and I are grateful to you for keeping photographers at bay but could you dump them somewhere else?'

7 August

A plan by rail chiefs to replace manned ticket-offices at smaller railway stations with machines only selling day-of-travel tickets — thereby denying passengers the opportunity to buy high-discount fares in advance — led to fears of more rural station closures.

'He says: Are we going anywhere near a mainline station so as he can buy a ticket?'

8 August